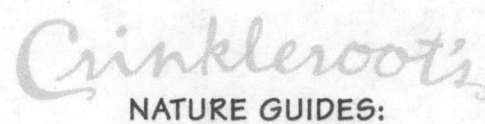

NATURE GUIDES:

I Was Born in a Tree and Raised by Bees
Crinkleroot's Book of Animal Tracking
Crinkleroot's Guide to Knowing Butterflies & Moths
Crinkleroot's Guide to Knowing the Birds
Crinkleroot's Guide to Knowing the Trees
Crinkleroot's Guide to Walking in Wild Places
Crinkleroot's 25 Birds Every Child Should Know
Crinkleroot's 25 Fish Every Child Should Know
Crinkleroot's 25 Mammals Every Child Should Know
Crinkleroot's 25 More Animals Every Child Should Know

FOR MY SISTER, DONNA

SIMON & SCHUSTER BOOKS FOR YOUNG READERS
An imprint of Simon & Schuster Children's Publishing Division
1230 Avenue of the Americas, New York, New York 10020

The text for this book is set in Bookman Medium.
The illustrations are rendered in watercolor.
Printed and bound in the United States of America
First Edition
1 3 5 7 9 10 8 6 4 2

Library of Congress Cataloging-in-Publication Data
Arnosky, Jim.
Crinkleroot's guide to knowing animal habitats
by Jim Arnosky.—1st ed.
p. cm.
Summary : Introduces different wildlife habitats,
including wetlands, woodlands, cornfields, and grasslands.
ISBN 978-1-4814-2599-5
1. Habitat (Ecology)—Juvenile literature. [1. Habitat (Ecology)]
I. Title.
QH541.14.A75 1997 591.5—dc20 96-19226

Crinkleroot's
GUIDE TO KNOWING
ANIMAL HABITATS
BY JIM ARNOSKY

Simon & Schuster Books for Young Readers

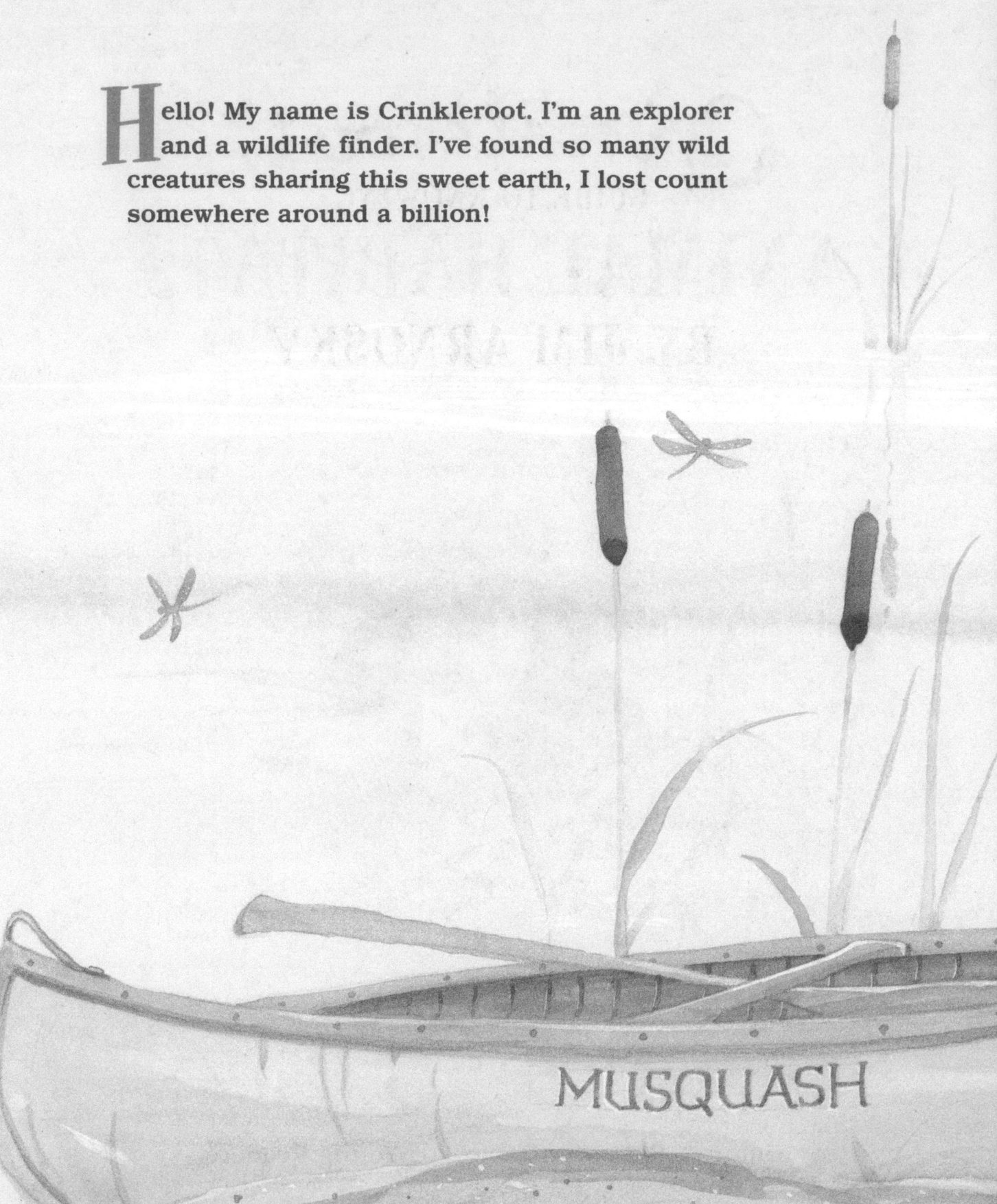

Hello! My name is Crinkleroot. I'm an explorer and a wildlife finder. I've found so many wild creatures sharing this sweet earth, I lost count somewhere around a billion!

MUSQUASH

I see so many wild critters because I know where they all live. The natural places where wild animals live are called habitats.

I'm going to visit lots of different wildlife habitats. You can come too!

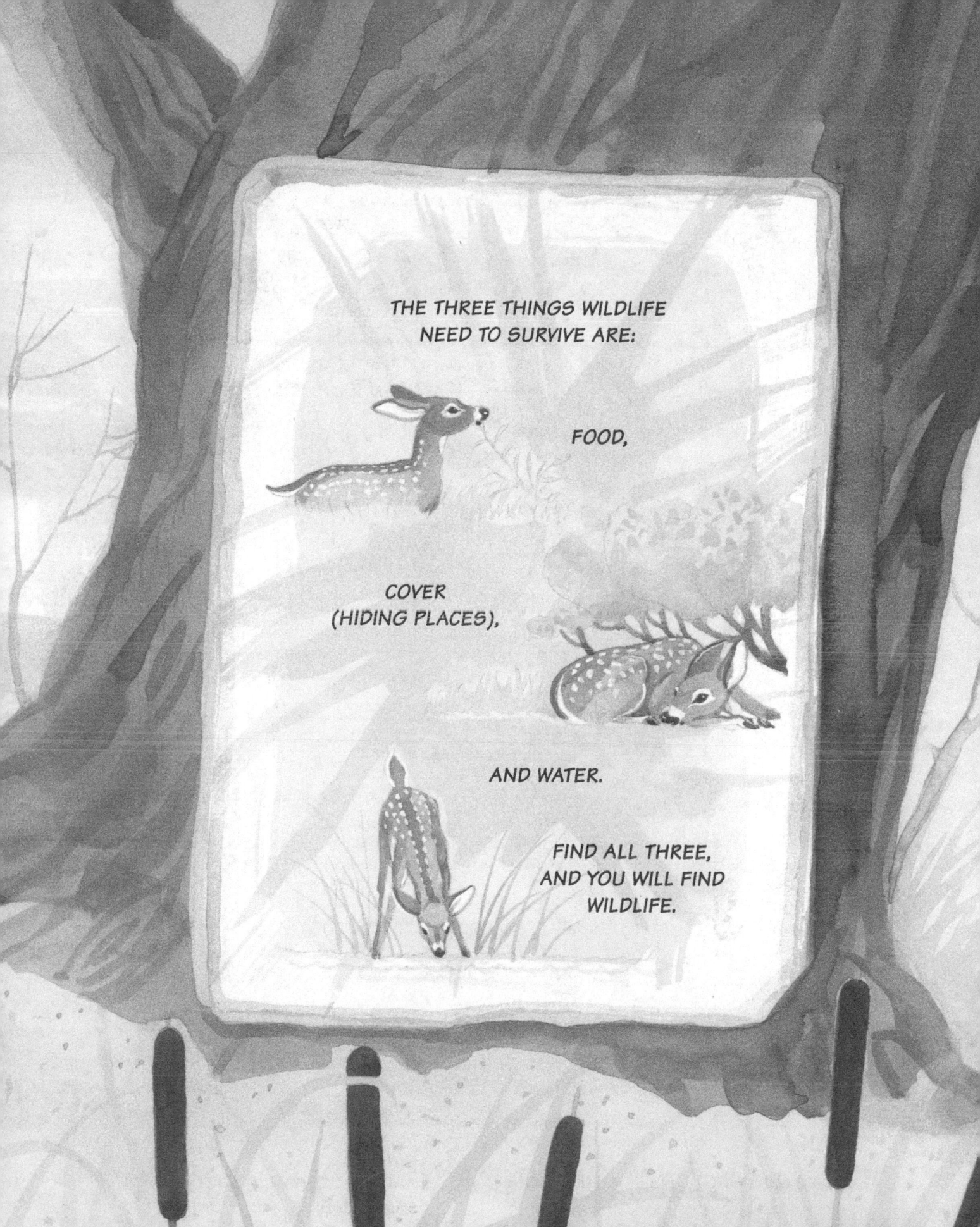

The first place I want to show you
is a watery place, or wetland.

CROSS SECTION OF A WETLAND:

MUD
WATER TABLE (WATER LEVEL IN SOIL)
SAND, PEBBLES, AND STONES.

A wetland is any place where water is near, at, or just above the surface of the ground. You may have a tiny wetland in your own backyard where the soil is always moist and the grass grows more lush.

NOTE: SOME TYPES OF WETLANDS ARE NOT FIRM ENOUGH TO WALK ON. THE BEST WAY TO OBSERVE MOST WETLANDS IS IN THE COMPANY OF AN ADULT AND FROM THE SAFETY OF HIGHER GROUND OR A STURDY BOARDWALK.

The three most common wetlands are marshes, swamps, and bogs. A marsh is full of tall grasses, cattails, and reeds. Here water is above ground in many spots.

CANADA GEESE

GREAT BLUE HERON

MERGANSERS

PAINTED TURTLE

RED-WINGED BLACKBIRD

MALLARDS

BULLFROG

MUSKRAT

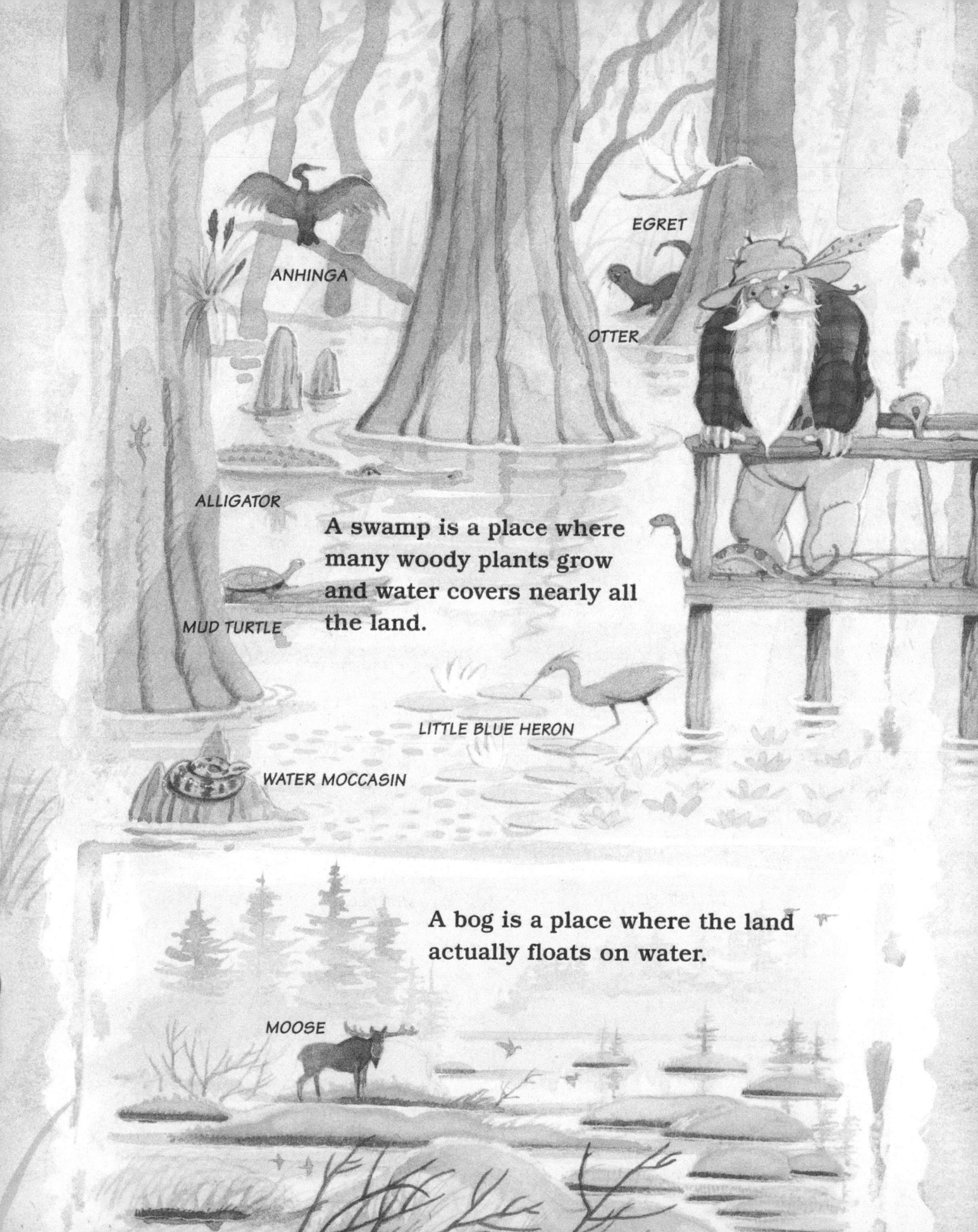

ANHINGA

EGRET

OTTER

ALLIGATOR

A swamp is a place where many woody plants grow and water covers nearly all the land.

MUD TURTLE

LITTLE BLUE HERON

WATER MOCCASIN

A bog is a place where the land actually floats on water.

MOOSE

The shallow water of any wetland is a world of plants, rocks, sand, and sunken trees.

SUNFISH

NEWT

DAMSELFLY
LARVA

FRESHWATER
MUSSEL

WATER
BOATMAN

CRAYFISH

DRAGONFLY
LARVA

MINNOWS

MADTOM

It is a rich weedy habitat for underwater wildlife.

PICKEREL

SNAPPING
TURTLE

In a woodland, tree trunks, stems, and branches criss-cross and overlap. It takes sharp eyes to pick out even the noisiest creatures, like hammering woodpeckers or chirping red squirrels. But make no mistake! Any woodland is habitat for a variety of wildlife. For every animal you hear or see, there are many more hiding.

WHITE-BREASTED NUTHATCH

RED
SQUIRREL

GREAT
HORNED
OWL

In the woods, animals may be living high in the treetops, in middle branches or trunks, or on the woodland floor.

See if you can find the wildlife living in this little patch of woods. (I'll give you a hint: there are twenty-four in all. Twenty-seven if you count walking stick, Sassafrass, and me.)

Climb aboard my old jalopy! There are some interesting places I want to show you that are miles apart. Along the way, we're sure to spot some wildlife near the road.

RING-NECKED PHEASANT

CROWS

DEER

WOODCHUCK

Rabbits, deer, woodchucks, and other normally shy animals come out to the roadsides to feed on lush green plants growing in the open sunlight.

Roadsides are also hunting grounds for hungry crows, hawks, and kestrels.

RED-TAILED HAWK

KESTREL

35 MPH

NATURE

RABBIT

Our first stop is a farmer's cornfield. Cornfields provide an ever-changing habitat for wildlife. In the spring gulls, swallows, and bluebirds feed on beetles, grubs, and earthworms unearthed by the farmer's plow.

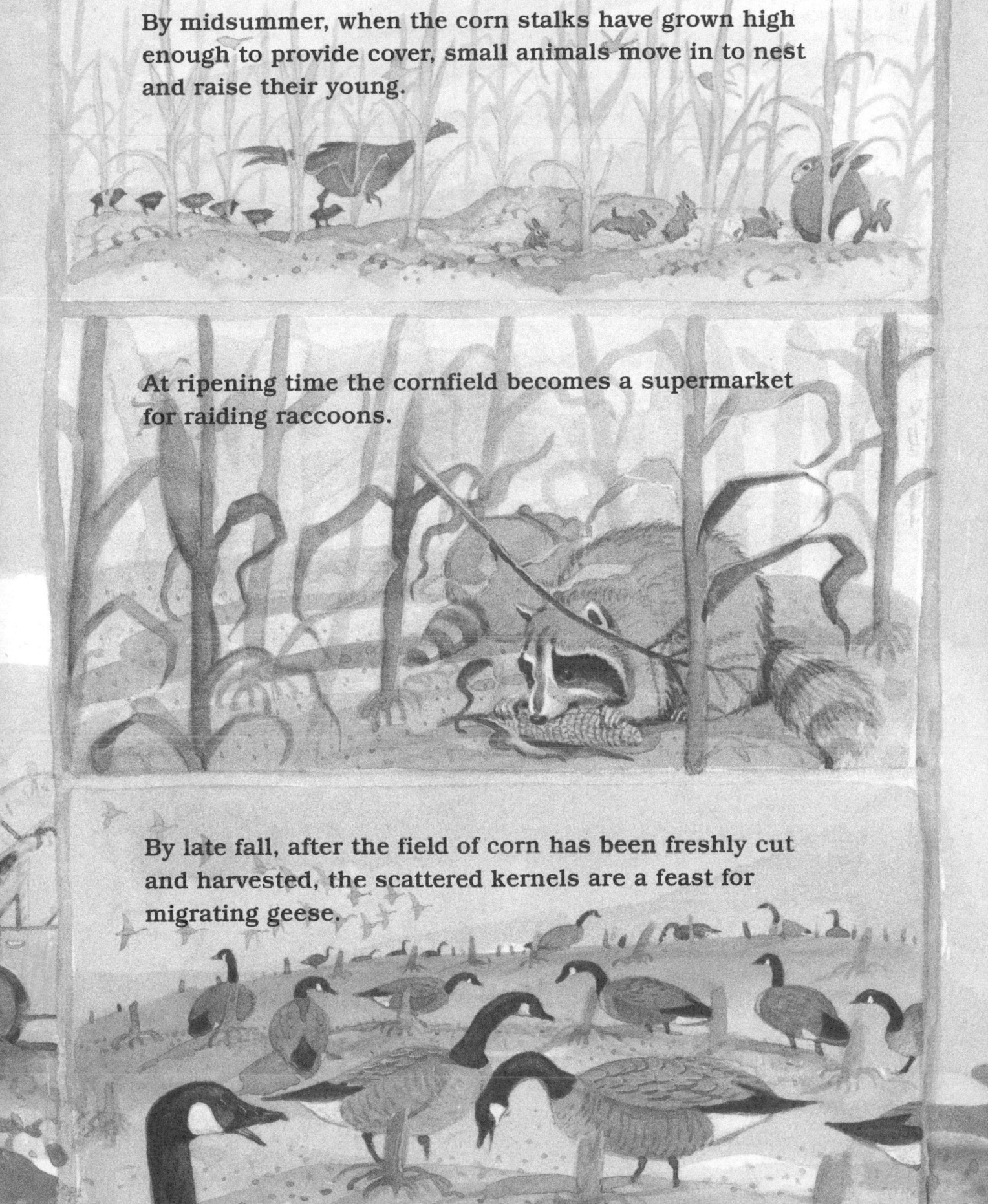

By midsummer, when the corn stalks have grown high enough to provide cover, small animals move in to nest and raise their young.

At ripening time the cornfield becomes a supermarket for raiding raccoons.

By late fall, after the field of corn has been freshly cut and harvested, the scattered kernels are a feast for migrating geese.

BURROWING OWL

PRAIRIE DOGS

MOST SMALL GRASSLAND ANIMALS ARE BIRDS OR BURROWERS—OR BOTH!

From small hillside meadows to vast rolling plains, grasslands are wide open spaces where wildlife can thrive.

GOLDFINCH

MONARCH BUTTERFLY

TICK

WHEN WALKING IN GRASSLAND, STOP TO CHECK YOUR CLOTHES FOR TICKS. TICKS ARE NUMEROUS IN TALL GRASS.

YOU'LL FIND MORE KINDS OF INSECTS AND SPIDERS IN GRASSLANDS THAN IN ANY OTHER HABITAT.

PRONGHORN ANTELOPE

BISON

THE LARGEST INHABITANTS OF GRASSLANDS ARE GRAZING ANIMALS.

At first, grassland looks void of anything but waving green stems. But take time to really look and you will discover something wonderful.

THE BADGER IS A GRASSLAND PREDATOR THAT CAN DIG DOWN TWELVE FEET TO CATCH BURROWING PREY.

THE COYOTE AND RED FOX ARE OPEN COUNTRY PREDATORS THAT OFTEN SHARE THE SAME HUNTING GROUNDS.

SPIDER

GRASSHOPPER

VOLE

WOODCHUCK

VULTURE

Wherever the road leads, you will find wildlife living there. Even the hottest, driest places can be home to animals. In the drylands, wildlife find cover behind sage brush and cactus, beneath rock ledges, or for some, simply by digging in and covering up with sand. Succulent plants provide both food and water. And for predators, there is prey.

HERE IS A SAMPLING OF THE MANY WILDLIFE SPECIES THAT INHABIT DRYLANDS FROM SAGE BRUSH COUNTRY TO DESERT SANDS.

MULE DEER

ARMADILLO

KANGAROO RAT

JACKRABBIT

DIAMONDBACK RATTLESNAKE

ROADRUNNER

COLLARED LIZARD

BROAD-BILLED HUMMINGBIRD

HORNED LIZARD

ELF OWL

RAVEN

NATURE

PIKA

Learn to recognize the different wildlife habitats, from lowlands to mountains, wetlands to drylands. Don't be fooled by how small a place may be. Some wild critters get by in surprisingly little space—a bit of brush, a swampy puddle, a pile of rocks, a tiny woodlot, or a lone cactus.

Well now! I told you we'd cover a lot of territory and we did! I counted over eighty different wildlife species on our trip. How many did you count? I hope you enjoyed the journey. I did. So did Sassafrass. She always likes riding in the old jalopy. We'll see you soon. Until then, remember, wherever you go, you share the world with wildlife.

BIGHORN
SHEEP

Crayola

I feel
Craymoji

Puffy Sticker and Activity Book

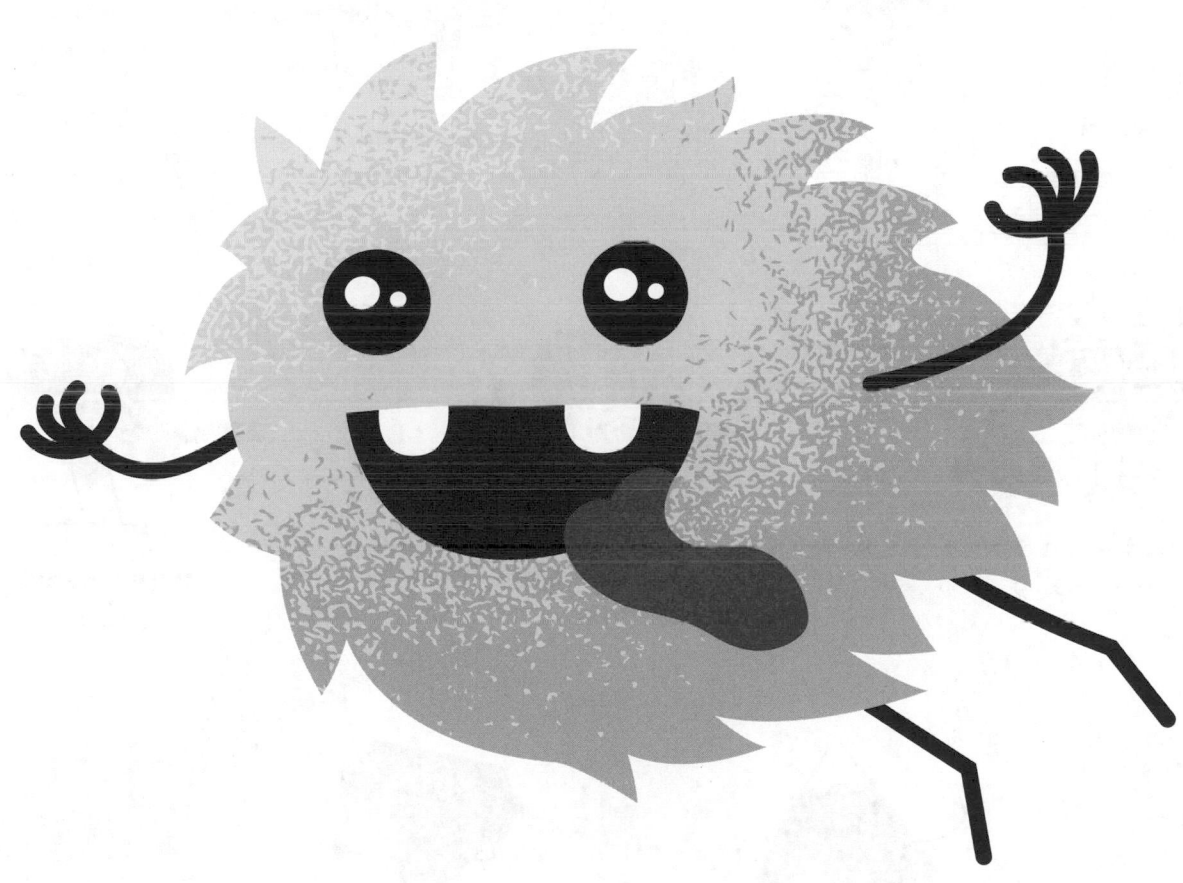

BuzzPop

Meet the Craymojis

Craymojis are wonderful friends who use their colors to share their feelings.

**Razzmatazz
is bold.**

**Sunset Orange
is relaxed.**

**Unmellow Yellow
is wild.**

**Tickle Me Pink
is silly.**

**Macaroni and Cheese
are cozy.**

**Granny Smith Apple
is wise.**

**Robin's Egg Blue
is calm.**

**Purple Heart
is proud.**

**Mountain Meadow
is happy.**

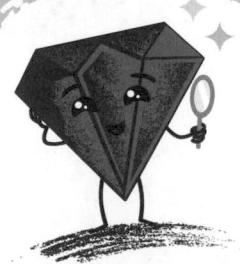

**Bluetiful
is confident.**

Connect the Craymojis

Match the Craymoji to its emotion!

OUTGOING

COZY

CONFIDENT

HAPPY

CALM

PROUD

ENERGIZED

Check answers on page 24!

Think Tickle Me Pink

How would you describe Tickle Me Pink?
Find the three words that are in the same color and write them
in the spaces at the bottom of the page.

STYLISH **FUN** FRIENDLY

WILD **HAPPY**

SILLY **PROUD**

HONEST **RELAXED**

FIERCE OPTIMISTIC CUDDLY

PLAYFUL COZY

_____   _____   _____

4

Check answers on page 24!

Tickle Me Pink is so happy and silly, and loves to laugh.
What's making this Craymoji laugh so much?
Draw it here!

Let's Go Unmellow Yellow

Pick the correct path to follow Unmellow Yellow
on another wild and daring adventure!

Check answer on page 24!

Unmellow Yellow and Extra Bold

Find the three things that are different between the two pictures below and circle them.

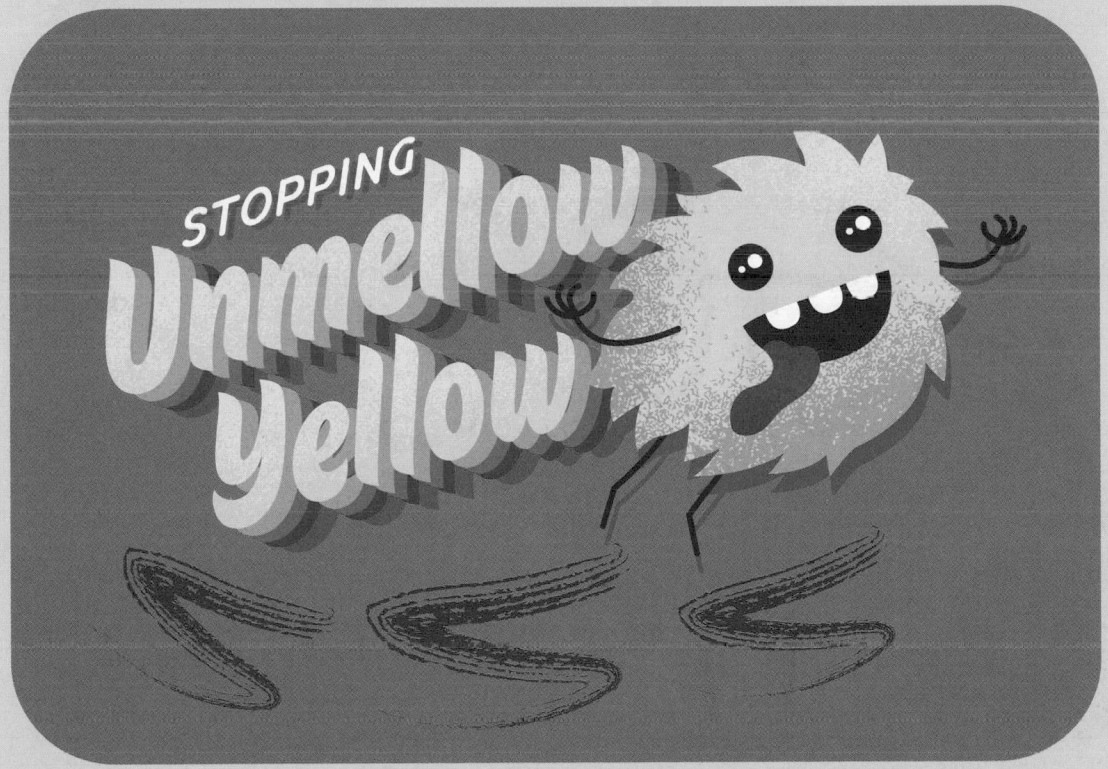

Check answers on page 24!

Unscramble the words to describe this Craymoji.

SEIW _ _ _ _

LAYHETH _ _ _ _ _ _ _

TRIVACEE _ _ _ _ _ _ _ _

8

Check answers on page 24!

Granny Smith Apple Is My Secret Ingredient

Can you add the missing words to complete this image?

Check answers on page 24!

Who's the Craymoji who always looks so good?
Connect the dots to find out!

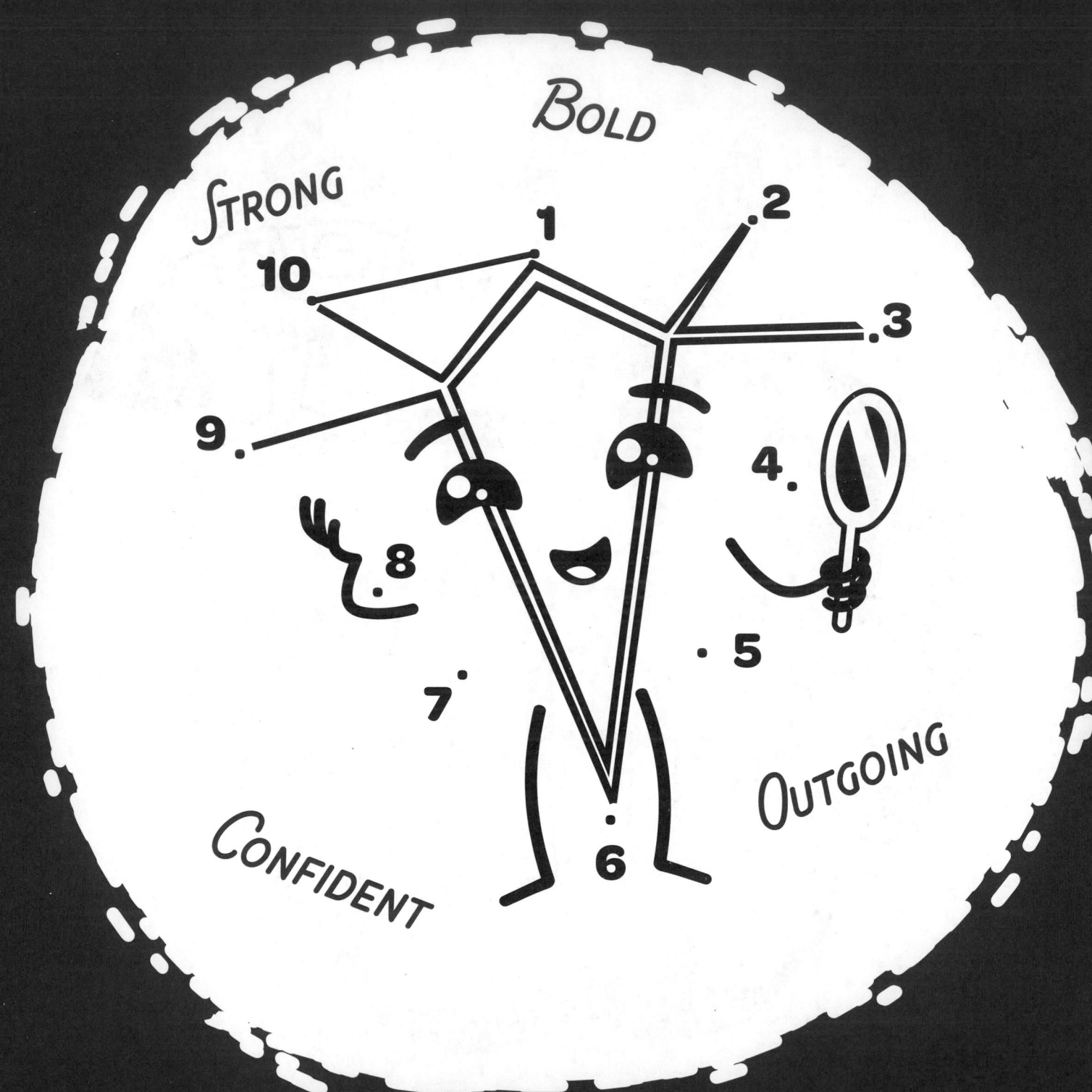

Check answer on page 24!

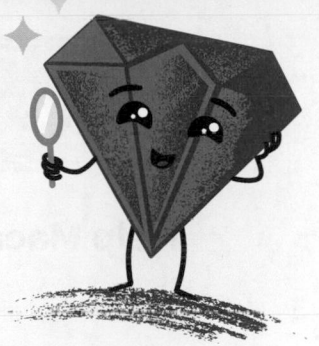

Bluetiful Vibes Only

Find the following words!

BLUETIFUL	**LOOK**	**BOLD**
OUTGOING	**CONFIDENT**	**STRONG**
YOU	**MORE**	**DAY**

```
H I R T W R A Q A M O R E B L E S Q O O
O R S F E T S N M E S L O T I A X E I U
P T O K P N Y E H C I P C Z S J E A T T
Q R F C E O Q B Z F T O G G N Q B R L G
H E N O B R V C C T A A P Q A W X W G O
M E R N H M Q X X E J X R S Q Y U A K I
G O V F D L H L K O P E T E R W S Q I N
F Q R I S E R R h B F H O A N K V H P G
L W B D X R B L U E T I F U L A T A K A
M W R E D J W M P I Q I T O R Q S Q P A
U K F N G X E A L R E I L R K V T Q T Q
Q G M T R M A B Y O R N F S O R N D A Y
P L K B O H L G J K E W Z E A D X A M T
R W P Q N I A R N B T U S F E O Z I A C
U M O I V A V A O L T S E D H R O E R O
E B N R B S T R O N G F B V A N L F L M
M O G N A R T P R S Q O C R J E O T T B
D L I O Q L M G O E Q O Q T G A O P O H
B D T O Q S N R F L E R E L T V K Y O U
```

Check answers on page 24!

Macaroni and Cheese = Happiness

Help Macaroni get to Cheese at the center of the maze
so they can be cozy together!

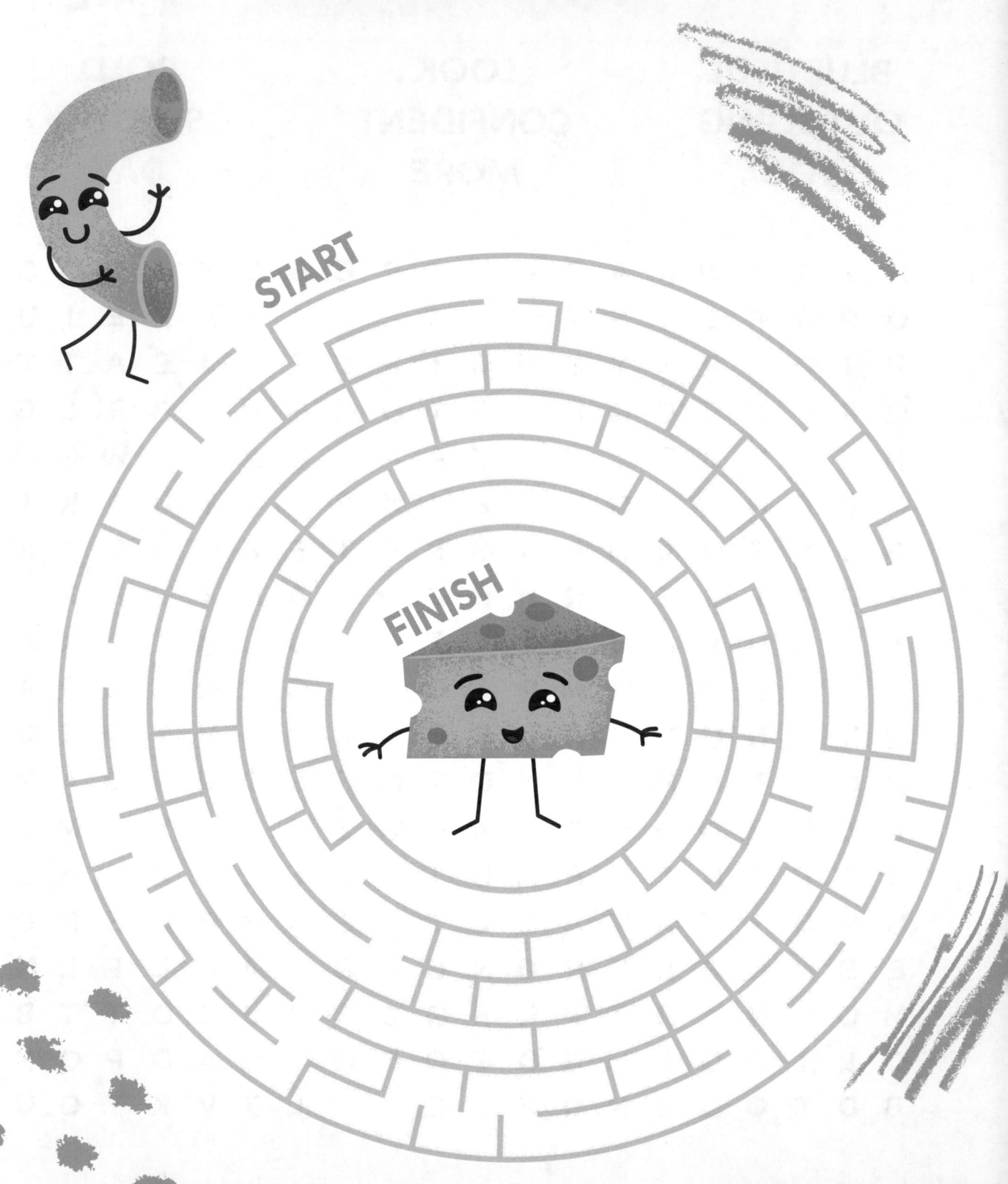

START

FINISH

Check answer on page 24!

It's a Macaroni and Cheese Kind of Day

One set of these buddies doesn't match any of the other pairs.
Find it and circle it.

Check answer on page 24!

Purple Heart won all the stars below! How many are there?

Write your answer here: _____

Check answer on page 24!

Purple Heart-Inspired

Purple Heart won a prize! What does it look like?

Draw it here.

Circle which of the two images will complete the pattern!

A.

B.

RAZZ MA TAZZ -TIC!

Check answers on page 24!

Trace the dashed lines of these bold letters.

Robin's Egg Blue looks so calm when sleeping. Draw what this Craymoji is dreaming about.

DREAMING IN ROBIN'S EGG BLUE

Robin's Egg Blue Makes Me Smile

Use a letter from each of the three words below to complete the fourth word at the bottom of the page. And keep smiling!

CALM

POSITIVE

CHEERFUL

OPTI_IS_I_

Check answer on page 24!

**Sunset Orange likes to relax.
Finish the scene below to show where
this Craymoji is relaxing.**

Complete the two shapes below to be as happy as Mountain Meadow.

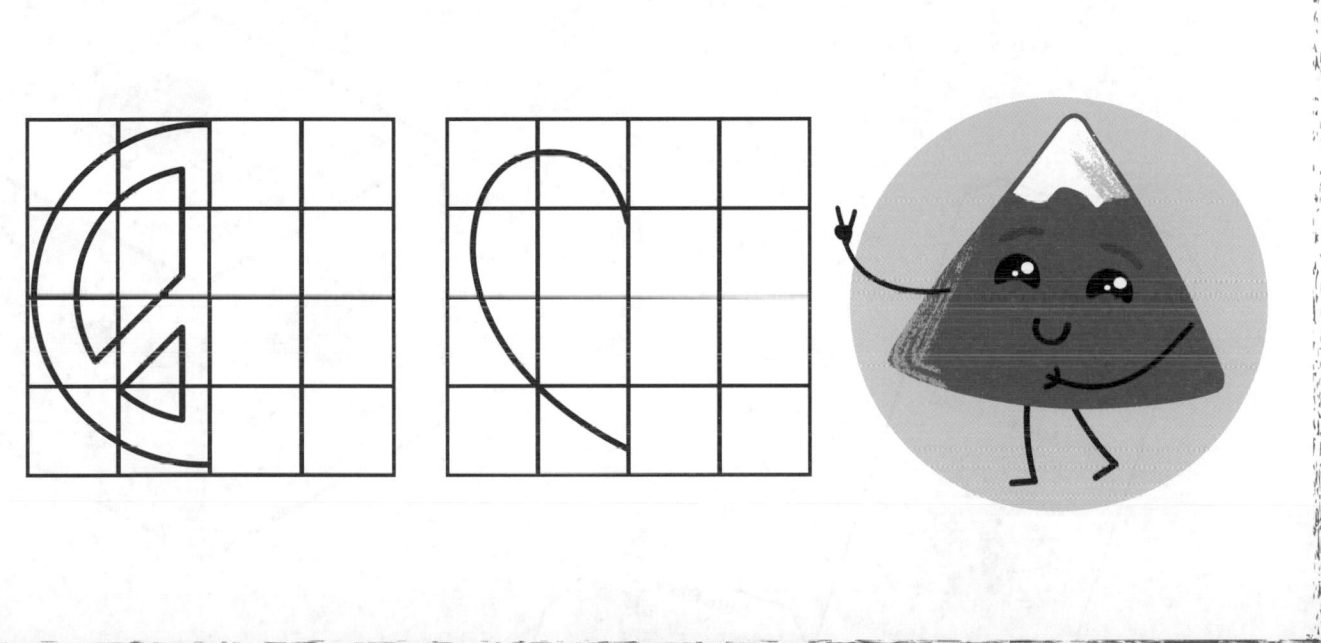

Check answer on page 24!

How to Use Your Press-outs

Make Your Mood Cube

1. Press out the Mood Cube template and fold along the dotted lines.
2. Add glue to the tabs where it says "Glue Here."
3. Fold your template into a cube, holding it together with the sticky tabs.
4. Wait for the glue to dry.
5. Now you're ready to play! Roll the cube and see what mood you're in today!

Craymoji Door Hanger

1. Press out the door hangers from the press-out pages.
2. Add glue to the back of each one and press them together.
3. Wait for the glue to dry.
4. Hang the door hanger to let people know when you're asleep or ready to play!

Match the Mood!

1. Mix or shuffle your Craymoji cards and place them facedown on a flat surface.
2. The first player turns over two cards. If the cards match, the player keeps them and gets another turn.
3. If they don't match, the player turns them back over so that the cards are facedown again. Then it becomes the next player's turn.
4. Repeat turns until all the pairs have been found and collected. The player with the most pairs wins!

Answer Key

Page 3:

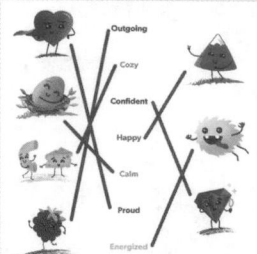

Page 4: HAPPY, PLAYFUL, SILLY

Page 6: Path 2

Page 7:

Page 8: WISE, HEALTHY, CREATIVE

Page 9: GRANNY and DAY

Page 10:

Page 11:

Page 12:

Page 13:

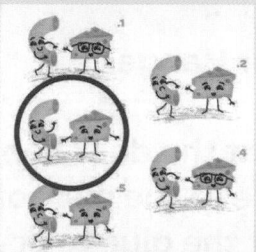

Page 14: 4

Page 16:

A.   B. -TIC!

Page 19:
CALM POSITIVE CHEERFUL OPTIMISTIC

Page 21:

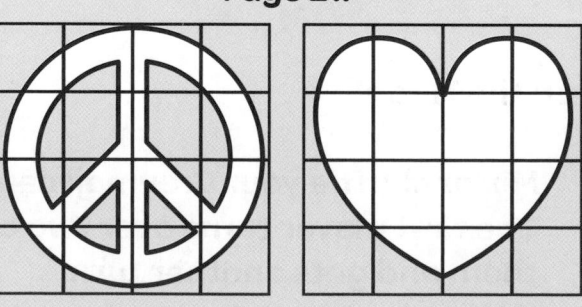